Te KAWA o te MARAE

A guide for all marae visitors

Wena Harawira

Contents

Introduction

For centuries marae were the heart of Maori communities but when Europeans came to this land, things changed. The marae then became a meeting place for other people as well as the Maori.

Many Pakeha and other non-Maori New Zealanders are interested in learning and understanding about the Maori people and their culture by visiting marae.

Maori people have made a special effort to welcome and encourage these visits.

If you're visiting a marae, it's a good idea to know something about its customs and rules. Then you can show your respect to your Maori hosts, avoid doing or saying anything wrong, and have a great time while you're there!

The marae in Maoridom

Firstly we should begin by asking what is a marae and what do people do there?

The marae and the events that take place there are of great importance to the Maori.

It's a place where Maori people can gather to celebrate special occasions like weddings, reunions and birthdays. It's a meeting place where people can talk or argue, care for guests, pray and weep for their dead.

A marae needs people and people need a marae. The tangata whenua (the people of the land or the hosts) are responsible for the care of their marae. And they take special care of visitors. There's a well-known Maori saying among Maori about this:

He aha te mea nui?

What is the greatest thing?

He tangata,	It is people,
He tangata,	It is people,
He tangata!	It is people!

Maori believe a marae is their turanga-waewae (a standing place), a place where they know they belong. You could say it's their home. Maybe you've heard people say with a sigh of relief, "Thank goodness I'm home." Everything is familiar — the faces, the surroundings, the noises, the talking. It's a home where they belong and can truly relax.

Organising a marae visit

Before going to a marae it's important to understand the kawa (rules) as this varies from one tribe to another and from one marae to another.

It's okay to feel a little unsure about your first visit to a marae. Don't expect to understand a marae after one visit. Because just like getting to know a person, it takes time.

Prepare yourself for your visit. Mattresses, sheets and pillows are provided by the marae but you need to bring:

▲ blankets or a sleeping bag
▲ pyjamas
▲ a towel and toilet gear
▲ a change of clothing
▲ a jersey, raincoat or sun hat (depending on the weather)
▲ socks or slip-on shoes (that are easy to remove)

5

On the marae

▼▼▼

Tangata whenua
Hosts of the marae

The tangata whenua are the local people who belong to the marae. They decide the kawa of the marae: what meetings can be held and when they might best be held; and who should be doing what on the marae.

They prepare the marae for guests by making sure there's plenty of food on hand, doing the work in the kitchen, dining room, meeting house and grounds, and forming the welcome party at the marae.

There is no particular boss on a marae and, to a visitor, it's probably amazing that large groups of people can be so easily welcomed, fed and cared for, with little fuss and bother.

During a marae visit, guests are able to help the tangata whenua on the marae.

They're free to move on any part of the marae. They can help in welcoming more visitors, perhaps join the pae (speakers' platform), even help out with the dishes!

Children can go and play anywhere on the marae. But they should stay away from the marae atea when the welcome or powhiri is being held. Adults on the marae become parents to all the children, taking care of them and making sure they don't do anything naughty!

Teenagers on the marae are expected to help out the adults. They can clear and set tables, serve meals, pour tea and coffee, wash and dry dishes and help the ringa wera (the cooks) prepare food.

Adults are the ringa wera. They order and deliver food, tend the fires or stoves, cook and serve or put a hangi down. They're in charge of making the marae ready for visitors and keep things running smoothly.

Kaumatua are the elders of the marae. Some are experts in Maori traditions like whaikorero (speeches) or whakapapa (genealogy). Some older women are good at waiata (song), others are expert in the karanga (call to visitors). The kaumatua front the marae to welcome visitors, take care that the kawa is followed and set an example to the young.

TANGATA WHENUA

Te huihuinga ki waho
Gathering outside the marae

When going onto a marae, manuhiri (visitors) gather outside the gates. It's a good idea to introduce yourself to other people who may join your group, either with a handshake, a kiss and hug or the hongi (pressing of noses).

Speakers for the manuhiri are chosen and the koha (gift or donation) is collected. The koha may be a gift of money and the amount given is left for each person to decide.

When the manuhiri move onto the marae, they should stay close together and move forward silently. In some areas, the men will usually go to the front, followed by the women and children. In other areas, the women or kuia will lead the manuhiri. The kaiwhakautu is a woman who returns the karanga for the manuhiri, and she usually stands to the front as they go onto the marae.

The giving of koha stems from the tradition of bringing gifts when visiting a marae. For the Maori, generosity and hospitality is a matter of honour. Giving rather than receiving is very important. Money is a modern form of koha, but Maori often used food as koha. Tribes would give food that was plentiful in their area but in short supply in their hosts' district. For example a group that lived in the bush would take preserved pigeons as their koha, while other tribes who lived by the sea would offer dried fish or shellfish.

Te wero
The challenge

Wero means "cast a spear". The wero was a traditional way of testing the visitors to see if they came in peace or in war. Today the wero is performed as a ceremonial challenge for very important visitors to the marae, and there can sometimes be up to three challengers.

The wero is always carried out by a man, and performed before the karanga is made. The challenger makes fierce faces and noises, and swings his taiaha at the visitors. This is a warning to visitors that the warriors of the tangata whenua are strong and ready to defend themselves if necessary!

The taki (challenge dart) is placed before the manuhiri and may be a small carved dart or a piece of greenery. The taki is always picked up by a male member of the manuhiri, and this shows the tangata whenua that the visitors arrive in peace.

The challenger who performs the wero is seen as a warrior of the god Tumatauenga or Tu. This god was the son of Ranginui, the Sky Father, and Papatuanuku, the Earth Mother, and was the protector and champion of warriors.

Tu fought with his brother Tawhirimatea when their parents were separated. Tawhirimatea had wanted his parents to stay together and attacked his brothers with winds and rainstorms to punish them. Tu was the only one brave enough to stand against Tawhirimatea, and he killed his brothers for refusing to help him. According to Maori belief, this set the scene for warfare: men make war now because Tu did so in the beginning.

11

Te karanga
The call of welcome

Women have a special role on the marae.
The karanga is the first expression of
welcome to a marae, and it is always
called by a woman — the kaikaranga.

A karanga can begin as a greeting to the manuhiri:

Haere mai ra,
Nga manuhiri tuarangi e,
Come forward,
Visitors from afar,
Haere mai, haere mai!
Welcome, welcome!

The karanga can also include a greeting to the spirits of the dead:

Mauria mai ra o koutou
tini mate,
Bring with you
the spirits of the dead,
Kia mihia,
Kia tangihia e.
That they may be greeted,
That they may be mourned.

The kaiwhakautu will return the karanga on behalf of the manuhiri. Her call may show who the visitors are and where they come from, and will also greet the tangata whenua and the spirits of the dead.

If there is no kaiwhakautu with the visiting group, don't worry! The tangata whenua may send a kaiwhakautu to join the manuhiri, or visitors may simply move onto the marae without replying to the karanga.

According to Maori legend, many Maori gods helped to make Hine-ahu-one, the first woman.

Tane, the god of forests, shaped her body from clay and his brothers and sisters hunted around the heavens to collect other parts for her body.

Her eyes were set into pieces of clouds to make the whites of her eyes. Tawhirimatea, the god of winds, gave her lungs to breathe, and another god plucked feathers from birds to make hair. Tumatauenga helped arrange the muscles of her body and Rongo, the god of peace, gave her a stomach. Her wairua (spirit), blood and power to breathe were given by Io, the supreme god.

When Tane breathed life into her form, Hine-ahu-one sneezed! It was a sign of life from the first woman created by the gods.

13

Te powhiri
The welcome

For the powhiri, the kaikaranga usually stands to the side of the tangata whenua. Those who take part in the powhiri include elders (men and women) and young people — in fact everyone who is on the marae when visitors arrive is free to join in.

During a tangi (a funeral) and especially when there is a tupapaku (a body) on the marae, the tangata whenua will hold small twigs of green leaves in each hand. These twigs are a symbol of mourning.

When the powhiri is being carried out the tangata whenua may perform actions to a chant. Below is one that likens the visitors' approach to the arrival of a canoe that is being drawn to shore:

Everyone who takes part in the powhiri is protected by the tapu of the marae.

The powhiri serves to ward off evil spirits, giving visitors safety as they move onto the marae.

Visitors will usually stop and stand for a short time to remember those who have died, when going onto the marae. Sometimes there is a call from the tangata whenua that the manuhiri have stood for long enough, or perhaps a final karanga, inviting the manuhiri to take their seats.

Speakers and senior members of the manuhiri sit in the front seats. Older women and those who'll support the kaikorero (speakers) sit close behind. Children are seated after the adults and if there are no seats left, they get to sit on the ground!

LEADER	PEOPLE	
Toia mai!	Te waka!	Pull up, the canoe!
Kumea mai!	Te waka!	Drag up, the canoe!
Ki te urunga!	Te waka!	To the resting place, the canoe!
Ki te moenga!	Te waka!	To the sleeping place, the canoe!

ALL	
Ki te takotoranga i	To the place where it will lie
Takoto ai, te waka!	At rest, the canoe!

15

Nga mihi, nga whaikorero
Greetings and speeches

The marae or marae atea describes the open courtyard in front of the meeting house.

The marae atea is used for welcoming guests and making speeches. The kai-korero or speaker moves back and forth or sideways across the marae atea, keeping a small distance between himself and the people he is talking to.

The order in which each speaker stands can change from tribe to tribe, and from area to area.

Sometimes all speakers for the tangata whenua will speak first. Then all speakers for the manuhiri will stand. This kawa is called paeke. Tribes in Northland follow this custom.

At other times, speeches start with one speaker for the tangata whenua. A speaker from the visiting group then stands and replies. Each side gets a turn until all the speeches are finished. This kawa is called tu mai tu atu. Tribes from the Waikato area follow this custom.

Speeches can take a long time, and it's easy to get fidgety and bored. It's okay to talk quietly amongst yourselves, but don't walk around or cross the marae atea while speeches are being held.

Almost all speeches are followed by waiata. Women — the "songbirds" — will usually begin the singing, standing to the side or behind the speaker. The waiata traditionally supports what the speaker has said. It can even add a little pizzazz!

In some areas the powhiri can take place inside the whare, especially during a tangi where the tupapaku lies inside the house rather than on the whakamahau (porch) or in the wharemate (mourning house). The same customs are followed, and the space within the whare between the tangata whenua and the manuhiri becomes the marae atea.

The last speakers during the powhiri have special duties.

The koha from the manuhiri is given by their last speaker, who places it on the ground at the end of his speech. It is then collected by the tangata whenua. Sometimes a woman may karanga after the laying down of a koha to show thanks.

The final speech during the powhiri is always made by the tangata whenua.

Nga mihi - whaikorero

Maori people believe the marae atea is the domain of Tu, the god of war, where bad feelings, arguments or nasty comments can be aired.

Some tribes believe women must be protected from this behaviour, and don't allow women to whaikorero or make speeches on the marae.

Some think it's unfair that only men are able to speak, but tribes like the Ngati Porou from the east coast of the North Island do allow their women to stand and whaikorero on the marae atea. Other Maori women believe that men speak on their behalf anyway and some even say that a man will only say what the women tell him to! If a speech is very important, everyone in a family can be involved in what should be said.

17

Hongi

The hongi is a traditional greeting of Maori people.

The pressing of noses during the hongi mingles the breath of two people in a show of unity. Sometimes the foreheads can also touch, as a way of sharing thoughts and emotions.

It is believed the first press is a greeting to the person you hongi with, a second press acknowledges ancestors, and a third press honours life in this world.

Maori people believe the mauri (life force) of the marae covers the manuhiri during the powhiri. By making the final speech, the mauri returns to the tangata whenua and isn't carried away by the manuhiri on their return home.

Once the speeches have ended, the manuhiri can move to the pae to hariru (shake hands) and hongi (press noses).

You may greet your hosts by saying "Tena koe" or "Kia ora", shaking hands then bending your head and pressing noses. Some people press noses twice, others press once. Whether you hariru, hongi, kiss or do all three, depends on how you would like to greet a person.

Greeting the tangata whenua removes the tapu of the welcome ceremony from the manuhiri, so they can join together with tangata whenua.

Waiata

The Maori people traditionally used songs as a way to record events in their lives.

Some waiata set down tribal history and great events, others were love songs, lullabies or laments for people who had died. Waiata were also a way of remembering the names of stars, place names or a family tree. They could also be used to greet people or insult them! Maori people found all sorts of reasons to compose songs.

There was a song about a man who had lost his fish hook and one about the wonderful food a woman had eaten.

The people of one Maori village even wrote a song about a pig. Pigs were scarce at the time and it was the first pig the villagers had ever owned. When it died, a special song was composed in its honour!

Te whare tipuna
The ancestral house

The meeting house of the marae can be called a whare tipuna or whare tupuna (ancestral house), whare whakairo (carved house), whare nui (large house), whare hui (meeting house), whare moe or whare puni (sleeping house), or whare runanga (council house).

The whare always has a name — this can be the name of an ancestor and the shape of the whare is believed to represent this ancestor's body.

Outside the whare, the tekoteko (carved figure) on the rooftop in front represents the head. The maihi (carved pieces sloping down from the tekoteko) are the arms.

Inside, the tahuhu or tahu (ridge pole), which runs down the centre of the whare, is the backbone. The heke or wheke (rafters) reaching from the centre of the roof are the ribs.

The poupou (carved figures) around the walls usually represent ancestors from the tangata whenua and other tribes. The pou tokomanawa (large poles) support the tahuhu and represent the link between Ranginui, the Sky Father, and Papatuanuku, the Earth Mother.

Some whare have woven panels of tukutuku (lattice work) with patterns.

Whakairo

Whakairo, the art of wood carving, was discovered by a man called Rua.
His son, Manuruhi, had disappeared one day while fishing, so Rua set out to find him. He dived into the ocean and soon found a large, carved meeting house that belonged to the god of the sea, Tangaroa. When Rua looked inside, he realised Tangaroa had changed Manuruhi into a wooden carving. That made Rua very angry! When Tangaroa's children returned to the house to sleep Rua grabbed Manuruhi and some other carvings and set fire to the house. He then stood by the door and killed some of Tangaroa's children with his patu as they rushed out. Some survived, like the stingray, the shark, the octopus and the snapper, and you still find them in the sea today. Rua returned home with the carvings, and he used these to teach Maori the art of wood carving.

These can represent stars (whetu), fish like the flounder (patiki) or the tears of the albatross (toroa).

On the heke, you may see kowhaiwhai (painted scroll designs) or folk art —

Pukana

If you look closely at the poupou (carved figures) inside a whare you'll notice that many have wide, bulging eyes!
These represent the eyes of the owl or ruru. The owl is seen as a wise bird in the stories of many people, including the Maori. When Rongo, the god of peace, built a sacred house of learning he buried an owl as a talisman beneath it. So the eyes of poupou pukana or glare wide-eyed — just like the owl — as a sign of that time.
It is said the pukana also mimics the owl glaring at the fantail when it annoys him with its constant and energetic flitting! So Maori performers of action songs and haka imitate both birds: making their eyes pukana to draw attention and look fierce, and swinging their poi in movements that resemble the flight of the fantail.

pictures of birds, flowers, people or events that have taken place. Most whare will also have photos hanging on the walls of those who have died.

Te whare kai
The dining room

Like the meeting house the whare kai is also named. It's here the tangata whenua show an important part of marae hospitality — feeding the manuhiri!

Elders and the speakers of the manuhiri lead the way into the whare kai. Manuhiri are always served their meals before any of the tangata whenua who may join them.

Grace is said before eating begins and a person from the tangata whenua will tap the table several times with a spoon or knife, to quieten the whare kai.

Don't dawdle over your food if there are others waiting for meals. The sooner one group leaves a table, the sooner the tables can be relaid for others. The ringa wera will eat their meal after all manuhiri have been fed and the dishes washed and dried.

Remember, never sit on a table — in the kitchen, dining room or any other room! It's very rude to sit on a surface where food is prepared or served.

Maori people believed it was important for a good husband to provide food for both his family and the whole village. Here is a story of how Kahungunu used food to win the love of a beautiful woman, Rongomaiwahine.

Fernroot was a valuable winter food for the Maori. So Kahungunu and his men gathered a large bundle of fernroot, and presented it to the people of Rongomaiwahine's village. Everyone thought he was so clever! Later he dived into the sea and brought up baskets filled with enough paua to feed the whole village. As a final trick, he stuck paua all over his body as he came up. Once more everyone cheered this great chief who was so clever at getting food!

Now Rongomaiwahine already had a husband, but this didn't stop Kahungunu wanting her. That night he ate a lot of paua, then sneaked over to where Rongomaiwahine and her husband slept. He pulled up the cloaks covering them and farted!

Kahungunu laughed quietly as he lay down. It wasn't long before the awful smell woke the couple up, and they argued, each blaming the other. When they settled down to sleep Kahungunu crawled back and did the same thing again. Once more the couple were woken by the horrible smell and argued! The noise of their fighting woke everyone up.

Kahungunu eventually married Rongomaiwahine and his deeds in winning the woman he loved went down in history!

Some traditional foods of the Maori have special meaning. Among the people of the Tuhoe tribe for example, only women can eat the meat of the kereru or pigeon, while the men are given the bones to suck or the soup made from boiling the birds.

It's thought that this custom allowed women one of the few sources of protein they needed to maintain their strength for having children.

Men were able to eat the meat of the kereru if it was cooked and preserved in the bird's fat, as they believed the mauri (life force) of the bird was removed if prepared this way.

TE WHARE KAI

Te whare moe
The sleeping house

There are separate areas of the whare moe set aside for manuhiri and tangata whenua. The manuhiri usually sleep to the right of the door, while the tangata whenua sleep to the left. Mattresses on both sides of the house nearest the door are left for elders or important people.

The whare is sometimes called Tane Whakapiripiri — Tane who draws people closest together. Beds can be arranged so that one pillow for each person is placed at the head of a mattress. This could mean that two people may share one mattress. Bags and coats can be left at the foot of the mattress, and your blanket can be laid where you will sleep.

Mattresses and soft pillows have a strange way of making some children want to play on them! In the box on page 25 are some things to remember inside the whare moe.

Most marae have karakia — a church service — in the morning and early evening. You may need to stand for some prayers or hymns, but you should sit up and not lie down through a service.

Don't be embarrassed if you snore; plenty of people do! In the morning, tidy up your blankets or pack your gear if you are leaving.

A great chief called Uenuku once fell in love with a fairy called Hinepukohurangi, the mist maiden.

Each night Hinepukohurangi would come down from the sky and sleep with Uenuku in his whare moe. But at dawn each day, her sister Hinewai would call to her and they would return to their home in the sky. Hinepukohurangi told Uenuku not to tell others about her until their first child was born, but Uenuku grew impatient. He wanted his fairy wife to stay with him and for his people to see how beautiful she was.

One night while she lay sleeping, he filled all the cracks in his whare moe with mud and grass, so the light would not shine through. Hinepukohurangi woke up at dawn but saw that the house was still dark, so she slept on. Outside Hinewai called to her sister, but Hinepukohurangi didn't hear her.

When the sun was high, Uenuku's people opened the door and Hinepukohurangi saw how she'd been tricked. She rose up into the sky and left Uenuku for ever. Uenuku searched all his life for his fairy wife but never found her. When he died, the gods took pity on him and changed him into a rainbow. And so Uenuku was reunited with Hinepukohurangi, and you may see them together today as a light mist around a rainbow.

- ▲ Don't jump around on the mattresses.
- ▲ Don't walk over people who may be lying down.
- ▲ Don't hog the pillows or mattress.
- ▲ Don't sit on pillows. The head is considered tapu and it's considered bad manners to sit on a pillow which is made for resting the head.

25

Tangi
Funerals

The tangi or tangihanga is a funeral service for a person before the tupapaku (body) is buried.

The Maori believe that the tupapaku should not be left on its own after death, so the family will gather to take the tupapaku from the undertaker to the marae or place where it will lie in the company of people until burial.

The coffin is sometimes left open and people may touch the tupapaku. Maori people believe that touching and crying over the tupapaku helps the pain of their loss.

People often travel long distances to attend a tangi to show their respect for that person and give their support to the dead person's family. Some may stay for a few hours or overnight and others may remain for two or three days.

All those who attend a tangi go through the powhiri, karanga and mihi, and speeches will be made directly to the tupapaku in the belief that the spirit does not leave the presence of the body until the burial.

The urupa or graveyard is sometimes located near the marae and is a special tapu place. On leaving the urupa, its tapu is removed by washing the hands in water. Many urupa have containers of water placed just outside the gate.

Maori people believe Hine-nui-te-po is a goddess who cares for and protects the souls of all people after their death.

One day Maui decided he would destroy Hine-nui-te-po so people would never die. A group of birds joined Maui as he crept up on Hine-nui-te-po who lay sleeping. But just as Maui prepared to enter her body and kill her, the fantail started to twitter loudly.

Hine-nui-te-po was woken by the chattering of the fantail. She saw what Maui was up to and killed him. So people have continued to die and their souls still return to Hine-nui-te-po in the underworld.

TANGI

Poroporoaki
The farewell

On the last day of your stay at the marae take your gear from the whare moe after breakfast. Or wait until after the hui whakamutunga (last session with the group together) or the poroporoaki (farewells and blessing).

The poroporoaki is as important as the powhiri and speeches of welcome. Here tangata whenua and the manuhiri will look back on the stay, show their thanks and approval, and say goodbye.

The manuhiri begin the ceremony with speeches of thanks to the tangata whenua, and finish off with songs. The tangata whenua have the chance to reply, then complete the poroporoaki with karakia. After a final hariru with their hosts, the manuhiri can leave.

Glossary

haere mai	come forward, welcome
haka	dance
hangi	food cooked in an earth oven
hariru	to shake hands
Hawaiki	the legendary homeland of the Maori
heke	the patterned rafters in a meeting house
Hine-ahu-one	the first woman created by the gods
Hine-nui-te-po	the goddess of death
Hinepukohurangi	the mist maiden
Hinewai	the water maiden
hongi	to press noses
hui	a meeting or gathering of people
huihuinga ki waho	gathering outside a marae
hui whakamutunga	the final gathering of a hui
Io	a supreme God
Kahungunu	a Maori ancestor of Hawkes Bay tribes
kai	food, to eat
kai karanga	a woman who gives the call of welcome to visitors
kai korero	a speaker
kai whakautu	a woman who returns the call of welcome
karakia	prayer
karanga	a call of welcome
kaumatua	elders
kawa	protocol, rules
kereru	native pigeon
koha	gift, donation
kowhaiwhai	patterns on rafters of the meeting house
kuia	elderly woman
maihi	bargeboards of a meeting house
mana	power, authority
manuhiri	visitors

Manuruhi	a man who was changed into a carving
Maori	the native people of Aotearoa (New Zealand)
marae	a traditional meeting place of the Maori
marae atea	the area between the tangata whenua and manuhiri during the welcome ceremony
Maui	a Maori hero
mauri	life force
mihi	to greet, a greeting
pae	main speakers and the place where they sit
paeke	order of speechmaking where all speakers from one group speak one after the other
Papatuanuku	Mother Earth
patiki	flounder
patu	a club
paua	abalone
poi	soft ball on a string
poroporoaki	farewell
poupou	carved panel in the meeting house
pou tokomanawa	carved post in the meeting house
powhiri	to welcome, the welcome ceremony
pukana	to glare wide-eyed
Ranginui	the Sky Father
ringa wera	hot hands, the cooks and workers of a marae
Rongo	god of peace
Rongomaiwahine	an ancestress of Hawkes Bay tribes
ruru	native owl
tahuhu, tahu	the ridge pole of the meeting house
taiaha	a wooden spear
taki	dart or twig used in the wero
Takitimu	the canoe of Hawkes Bay tribes
Tane	god of forests and life
Tangaroa	god of the seas
tangata whenua	people of the marae
tangi	to cry, funeral service
tangihanga	funeral service
tapu	sacred
Tawhirimatea	god of winds
tekoteko	the carved figure at the top of the meeting house
tipuna	ancestor
toroa	albatross
tukutuku	woven panels in the meeting house
tu mai tu atu	order of speeches where hosts and visitors take turns speaking
Tumatauenga	god of war
tupapaku	the body of a dead person

turangawaewae	standing place where a person belongs
tutakitanga	to meet
Uenuku	Maori ancestor who became a rainbow
urupa	cemetery
waiata	song, to sing
wairua	spirit
wero	challenge
whaikorero	to make a speech
whakairo	carving
whakamahau	porch of a meeting house
whakapapa	genealogy
whare	house or building
wharehui	meeting house
whare kai	dining room
wharemate	house of mourning
whare moe	sleeping house
whare nui	the main house
whare puni	sleeping house
whare runanga	council house
whare tipuna	ancestral house
whare whakairo	carved house
wheke	rafters of a meeting house
whetu	stars

GLOSSARY

Reed Publishing (NZ) Ltd
Te Karuhi tā tāpui o Reed (Aotearoa)

Established in 1907, Reed is New Zealand's largest
book publisher, with over 300 titles in print.

For details on all these books visit our website:
www.reed.co.nz

ISBN 1 86948 960 8

First published in 1997 by Reed Children's Books, an imprint of
Reed Publishing (NZ) Ltd, 39 Rawene Road, Birkenhead, Auckland.
Associated companies, branches and representatives throughout the world.
Reprint 1997, 2000, 2004, 2005
© Wena Harawira, text
© Holger Leue, photographs pp 6, 7, 20(top), 22, 25
© Martin Barriball, photographs pp 11, 28
© Don Stafford, photographs pp 8, 12, 15, 18
© Stephen Robinson, photograph p 4

Designed by Clair Stutton

Printed in China